Straight Out of View

To John,

Who is going forth
into the beautiful world
of islands and deserts
to seek his poetic
fortune. All good
chances be yours!

Best
Joyce

Barnard New Women Poets Series

Edited by Christopher Baswell and Celeste Schenck

Joyce Sutphen

Straight Out of View

Beacon Press
Boston

Grateful acknowledgment is made to the editors of the journals in which these poems
first appeared:

"In Praise of Unlovely Voices," *Loonfeather*, vol. 12, no. 2, Fall 1991–Winter 1992.

"Reading Sylvia Plath in London" and "Somewhere, Close to Dover Beach," *Cape Rock*,
Spring 1992.

"Straight Out of View," *Scread*, vol. 1, no. 4, 1992.

"Lunar Landing," *Scread*, vol. 2, no. 2, 1992.

"Dreaming You Out of Honduras" and "The Beginnings of Philosophy,"
Spoon River Poetry Review, Spring 1993.

"How the Puritans Took London," *Slant*, Spring 1993.

"Coil and Halt" and "After Visiting the Oracle," *Birmingham Poetry Review*,
Summer 1993.

"Death Becomes Me," *Poetry*, July 1994.

"A Kind of Deliverance," *Visions International*, Summer 1994.

"Potato Meditation," *Lake Region Review*, July 1994.

"Augie" poems and others, forthcoming in the *Minnesota Review*, Fall 1994.

Beacon Press
25 Beacon Street
Boston, Massachusetts 02108-2892

Beacon Press books
are published under the auspices of
the Unitarian Universalist Association of Congregations.

99 98 97 96 95   8 7 6 5 4 3 2 1

Library of Congress Cataloging-in-Publication Data

Sutphen, Joyce.
    Straight out of view / Joyce Sutphen.
        p.   cm. — (Barnard new women poets series)
    ISBN 0-8070-6825-X (pbk.)
    1. Farm life — Minnesota — Fiction. I. Title. II. Series.
PS3569.U857S77 1995
811'.54 — dc20   94-24509
                                              CIP

for Sarah, Alicia, and Marna

Contents

Introduction

The poems in this book are poems in motion, poems in the act of transforming themselves even as the words fly onto the page. They are charged with energy and gloriously alive — from the title poem, "Straight Out of View," in which the poet's thoughts become as alive as birds, to the last, "Crossroads," in which

> *The second half of my life will be ice*
> *breaking up on the river, rain*
> *soaking the fields, a hand*
> *held out, a fire,*
> *and smoke going*
> *upward, always up.*

From "My Father's Farm" to Sylvia Plath's London, from childhood and earlier family women's memories to the Vietnam War, Joyce Sutphen's voice is the voice of a woman who has covered some territory.

Women's energy and passion have traditionally been seen as defects; women are always either "something else" or "too much," either Other or Excess. But when we place women at the center of inquiry, much that we have considered the norm in poetry becomes peripheral. Contemporary critical distinctions, for example, between traditional and avant-garde break down. The avant-garde has been concerned with how to "make it new" (in Pound's formu-lation), but when the "it" in question has been largely obliterated from the record, when it is, as Carolyn Kizer has said, "merely the private lives of one-half of humanity," we don't necessarily have to make it new. An untold story, an unexamined reality, an obliterated record is always new, because (as in *The Tempest*) "Tis new to thee."

Thus, while the contemporary male-centered sector of the avant-garde has seen its task as breaking down the traditional and stale ways of telling already twice-told tales, the contemporary women writers of what has been untold or ignored have tended to see three tasks, and not to place them in conflict with each other. The first has been simply to get the story told, get the information out, raise the undead woman, whether Lady Lazarus or Ophelia, and rearticulate her skeleton so she can walk again. The second has been to stake out a claim to the tradition, whether in poetry, in art, in architecture, in science: to assert our centrality to the art and our claim to the craft. And the final, and inevitable, task has been to transform what we touch. The transformation, of course, happens whether or not we consider ourselves avant-garde. As soon as any art or any record that has excluded us places us at its center, it is necessarily transformed. Muriel Rukeyser told us: "What would happen if one woman told the truth about her life? / The world would split open."

So, in the current vigorous renaissance of women's poetry, which is really just as much a renaissance of poetry, because it is a rediscovery of huge energies that have been lost, there is no dichotomy between traditionalist and experimental because the whole enterprise is transformative. The first task in any large historical or critical transformation is to get the names right, define the terms so that they are useful for the current enterprise. From this real world perspective, what has been called Other is actually Self, what has been considered marginal becomes central, and what has been called excess is actually generosity (what Dickinson called "possibility," "amplitude"). What women are now practicing, therefore, is not a poetics of excess or hysteria, but a poetics of generosity based on a transformative aesthetic.

Within this poetics, Joyce Sutphen's poems are a splendid new arrival. They are: traditional-experimental-lyric-accessible-complex-snapshots-moving pictures-poetry of language-poetry of witness: not in turn but all at once. "I knew it to be passionate," she says, speaking of the country out of which her poetry arises, "I knew it to be melodious," and this passion, this melody were always waiting outside the wings of poetry, even when "less is more" and a laid-back, ironic distrust of emotional commitment had become the norm. Even while conversing with the traditional voices or using the normative modes of what we might consider "mainstream," Sutphen revises them, changes them to serve her purpose. The conversation she has with the prior or current art gives her work texture and richness, as when an Eliot echo occurs to her on the rim of the Grand Canyon, Godot in the context of the Vietnam War, or Yeats in the context of "Tornado Warning." But this deep and literate immersion in prior art does not simply add richness. It is part of our time's complex process of feminist re-vision, by which we look at the traditions in which we have been acculturated and reexamine their unstated assumptions. So, in Sutphen's long series of London poems, she reexamines Plath and Hughes through the lens of Ophelia and Hamlet. Or, is it that she examines Ophelia and Hamlet through the lens of Plath and Hughes? Both, of course, and the reexamination takes place between poles of survival and suicide: Hamlet talked about suicide but Ophelia drowned herself. What happens when you place Plath and Ophelia at the center instead of the periphery of inquiry? Joyce Sutphen's poems happen, and they happen within this context of women's writing transforming the terms of poetry, the terms of culture.

Our culture is in motion now, and we don't know where it will come to rest. And so these poems, also, are about journeying "out of orbit," "straight out of view," outside the traditional boundaries even while using tradition to define them. The words of Sutphen's poem "Tornado Warning," as much about the country of poetry as they are about geographical location, tell us what her own poetry will be, "passionate," "melodious," "it [will] haunt / the memory," and be "singular / in its fury." But she is kind enough, in this singular fury, to provide us with instructions on how to read her, and that voice is one whose power and intelligence we will not want to do without once we have encountered it. "When I say things this clearly," she tells us, with perfect authority, "it is because I want to, / and when I am hard to understand, / it is because I am trying to speak your language." This is the voice of a poet whose excess has become generosity, whose alterity as a woman has become not marginal but central, the stuff of our times. How she gets from here to there, from Other to "out of orbit," is the pleasure, the art, and the sure-handed craft of these poems. Go out of view with her and you will not be disappointed.

Judith E. Johnson

Straight Out of View

Please Follow These Instructions

When I say things this clearly,
it is because I want to,

and when I am hard to understand,
it is because I am trying to speak your language.

If you hear the wind and the moon
in my voice, you must beware,

but when I speak of my childhood,
relax, you are safe then.

Sometimes I use words
that do not belong to me.

I hope you know whose they are.
I love to listen to the story

as I go along. You should
never tell me the ending.

One

Straight Out of View

I'm thinking of birds — not only white ones.
I'm thinking of all the birds in the *Golden Book of Birds*,
and of their nests, and the parts of the country
where they're likely to be found.

Tepees and moonlight,
I'm thinking of owls and winter roads,
of quiet smoke ascending,
twisting out of the skin cone.
Shadows, rocking against the fire.

Camomile and honey bees,
netted masks, and keeper's gloves.
Queens and drones and mysterious
dancing under the basswood leaves.
I'm thinking these wooden boxes,
the smooth-jointed edges of the hive,
are grayed like no other coffin.

Three-legged dogs and marshes,
tall reedy places where blackbirds wing.
Flaming eyes in the hillside,
the dragon kiln stoked, and breathing fire.
A black kiss smothers the clay.

I'm thinking of ink,
letters fading,
and words that are fragile.
They begin to fly away as birds do:
suddenly, straight out of view.

Double Exposure

She begins to see that she can bring
something brilliant back from the moment
made by the small click of her camera.

Tripod in the nylon night
she catches the moon arching
over the glowing rooftop.

Telephoto turns the earth
flat, and draws the distant river up
spreading its silver at the front steps.

Wide-angle bends the horizon into a circle;
one filter greens the forgotten fields,
another sears with a red eye.

She can make the yard light
into a star of trailing radiance,
and show the red tracks of someone's departure.

Later, lying on the bed, she
looks over to her double,
sitting in the chair.

She stretches out a hand
toward herself,
                          fingertips
barely touching.

The Farm

My father's farm is an apple blossomer.
He keeps his hills in dandelion carpet
and weaves a lane of lilacs between the rose
and the jack-in-the-pulpits.
His sleek cows ripple in the pastures.
The dog and purple iris
keep watch at the garden's end.

His farm is rolling thunder,
a lightning bolt on the horizon.
His crops suck rain from the sky
and swallow the smoldering sun.
His fields are oceans of heat,
where waves of gold
beat the burning shore.

A red fox
pauses under the birch trees,
a shadow is in the river's bend.
When the hawk circles the land,
my father's grainfields whirl beneath it.
Owls gather together to sing in his woods,
and the deer run his golden meadow.

My father's farm is an icicle,
a hillside of white powder.

He parts the snowy sea,
and smooths away the valleys.
He cultivates his rows of starlight
and drags the crescent moon
through dark unfurrowed fields.

Ways of Passing

This paper I come to is already slightly yellowed.
Lying on the shelf these months, it has had time
to dream itself back into the heart of a tree.
When the winds blow, the sheaf of broken wood moans.
Nothing is forgotten, only changed.

A pheasant flies up from the oat field.
Afterward, the horse remembers
the horror of that place:
the tattered beat of wing,
the ringed neck rising.

Crows, flying over the field
ripple their shadows
over the grainy sea.
Nothing of that remains.

Tornado Warning

That is not the country for poetry.
It has no mountains, its flowers
are plain and never poisonous,
its gardens are packed into blue mason jars.
There are no hedges bordering the roads, the sky
flies up from the ditches, loose in every
direction.
        Yet I knew it to be passionate,
even in its low rolling hills, where a red
tractor pushed through the oat field, cutting
down gold straw and beating a stream
of grain into the wagon trailing behind
in the stubble,
        I knew it to be melodious
in its birch woods, leaves shadowing
a stone-strewn river, the path along the bank
softened with pine needles, sunlight
woven in and out of branches, the many
colors of green, solid as a pipe organ's
opening chord,
        I knew it would haunt
the memory with its single elm,
where a herd of cows found shade
in the July heat, their bony tails
swinging the tufted bristle left and right
over the high ledge of a hip bone,

while at the horizon, a black fist
of storm came on, something not
to be averted, something singular
in its fury,
        as any blind heart knows.

Feeding the New Calf

The torso comes out slick and black,
after hoofs that are yellowed
like smoker's teeth, the back
two legs crossed over each other and
the head last, bunched over front legs.

Minutes later he is standing wobbly,
and the blunt mouth is sucking at my arm,
tongue rough as sandpaper, tickling along my
skin, ripping up the fine hair over my wrist.
I tie him with a rope of bailing twine,

Shake out a chunk of straw around him,
as the dust rises in the sunlit aisle. I pet
the wet coat that curls over his sharp
backbone, scratch ears that are thick as
tulip leaves, bent in the womb. Angus baby.

I think of the blue-gray afterbirth, like a shawl
he wore, now left in the gutter, of his mother,
how she groaned him out of her belly, her back
rocking back and forth in the metal stanchion,
the velvet fold of her throat on the cold cement.

After I pour the milk into a pail, I go to
where he is lunging on the rope, where he is
singing a desperate duet with his mother:
din of soulful mooing. I get him to suck

at the nipple, pulling his mouth over to it
with my hands dipped in his mother's milk,
my small solid fingers and not her warm udders,
no peach-veined bag to sink his cheek on.

The clouds sunk in his large brown eyes
float blue. He nudges me, hard.

Work

Fed the animal in me,
kept the flesh attached to bone,
when I would have walked
out of the air and into
my grave, willingly.
They taught me this well:
to keep moving continually,
never to idle my way into
the devil's workshop,
to go the extra mile
without being asked.
And what I felt,
my ripening crop of pain,
I let it go, shelled corn
through cracks
in the wagon's bed,
oats, threshed out into
streams of gold,
the flat satin of stem,
spun into mountains of straw,
and, most in my memory,
the fragrant bruise
of new mown hay
and my progression:
stoic
in the sharp stubble
left behind.

Potato Meditation

Tonight I am the potato peeling woman.
I stand by the porcelain sink,
looking into the farm yard,
at its gray silt heart,

At fence posts and barbed wire,
at bodies, black and white,
moving around the watering tank,
moving under the carrot-colored moon.

White mountains of cloud rise
over the shoulders of the shadowed woods.

I take up a potato and skim its skin away,
remembering how, with Easter's first
full moon, we went along the loamy furrows
dropping a chunk of potato, the eye cast up

To the heavens before we buried it deep.
Then, when the green unfurled, we mounded
the dirt around each plant, making
an expectant hill, a pregnant swell

Of sloping earth and waited the summer
to see what came from the field's cool womb.

Potatoes, small as marbles,
grew fat under the thickening canopy.
Stalk and leaves, each green roof sent life
to the mysterious brood nursing at its roots.

My Father Comes to the City

Tonight his airplane comes in from the West,
and he rises from his seat, a suitcoat slung
over his arm. The flight attendant smiles
and says, "Have a nice visit," and he nods
as if he has done this all before,
as if his entire life hasn't been 170 acres
of corn and oats, as if a plow isn't dragging
behind him through the sand and clay,
as if his head isn't nestling in the warm
flank of a Holstein cow.

Only his hands tell the truth:
fingers thick as ropes, nails flat
and broken in the trough of endless chores.
He steps into the city warily, breathing
metal and exhaust, bewildered by the
stampede of humanity circling around him.
I want to ask him something familiar,
something about tractors and wagons,
but he is taken by the neon night,
crossing carefully against the light.

St. Joe, The Angelus

And so the bells came and summoned us
up and down the street so main it had
no name, calling us from the green benches
in front of Linneman's General Store,
across the cyclone fence of playground
and the pipe-framed doors that rang even
like bells when they closed behind us,
the U-shaped bracket clanking into place
around the silvery pole. And so we walked,
still ringing down the street into Loso's,
painted red in its shady second-best
reputation, its wooden floors bent and
rippling toward the cash register,
and into the cool granite of the bank,
the green billiard light of the Midway,
the butcher's shop, and Jaren's Drugstore,
where a girl lingered at the magazine rack,
leafing out in lipstick dreams, her skin
tanning quietly, her fingernails glistening,
and then past the rolling red and white
stripe of the barbershop, where we learned
the word "leukemia" and across to where
the professor lived with his faint disdain
and his wild-haired children, all the way
over the broken edge of sidewalk and through

the arc of lawn sprinklers to my grandmother's
chrome table, the chip of gold and blue plate,
potatoes frying in butter, pickles in the dish,
and then exactly at the pause of noon, the Angelus.

Evening Angelus

I have forgotten the words,
and therefore I shall not conceive
of a mysterious salvation, I shall
not become a tall lily and bloom
into blue and white. Then what
oracular event shall appear on
my doorstep? What announcement
shall crowd me to a corner,
protesting an unworthiness,
which doubtless shall be believed?

But these are only bells we hear,
pulled down by the arms of the
drunken janitor, two fingers missing
on his left hand. And we have
climbed into that tower, its spiraling
wooden staircase creaking beneath our
feet. We have seen for ourselves
that it is only iron that rings, iron
swinging on an iron bar, the rough rope
threading down to the cold ground,
no death or holiness in
those hollow shells.

Refugee Dream

Last night you came to me:
friends, silent as river rocks;
brothers and sisters, brown as old photographs;
great aunts and cousins, riding in the ghosts of old cars.
All the dead, staring in slow confusion.

You arrived at suppertime
with the past in a bundle on your head.
"Leave it at the door," I told you,
and made soup while you set up your camp,
building a sadness into my bones.

Later, I moved the furniture
so that you could sleep, thick as leaves
on the carpet, and all the while I wondered
why you came to me, the least of your hopes,
as if to a faraway country.

In Black

The image that haunts me is not beautiful.
I do not think it will open into a field
of wildflowers; I doubt that it will take
wing suddenly, startling us into admiration.

It is one of those brutish facts of life,
the awkward nakedness of the memory when
it takes off its clothes and crawls
between the top and bottom sheet. Or rather,

It is my mother's memory that I carry,
pressed into my own: how at her grandfather's
funeral, his daughter — my mother's mother —
stood at an open door and cried, and then

The blood ran down her legs, gushing from
the womb where thirteen children had nestled,
and now, at once horrified and at ease with her
body's impropriety, they gathered all around.

This was the grandmother who lost three of those
thirteen, who hung a million baskets of wash,
who peeled a million potatoes, and splattered
her arms with the grease of constant cooking.

This was my grandmother who kept chickens,
who left her voice in the throats of all my aunts,

and was struck down in the cellar, legs twisted
beneath the fall and half her face stiffened.

Helpless until they found her, the jar
of canned fruit smashed on the cement.
And then at her funeral, I saw my mother's
tears, gliding ahead of me in a black limousine,
a procession not beautiful but haunting.

In Praise of Unlovely Voices

They make new tunnels in the ear:
voices that scrape open a path —
bent old women,
hanging on to a song with one finger.

They curl from the mouth:
a smoke that twists and circles,
disappearing quickly into the air.

They claw savagely at old wounds,
remember hidden scars,
say: did it ever end?

Brave voices that disdain praise,
and need no introduction,
laughing as they fall,
screaming as they rise.

Voices of misery,
voices of rage,
doing the rough work
of destruction, clearing
a place for something
to grow.

Burning the Woods of My Childhood

I am burning the woods of my childhood, tree by tree,
I am warming myself by the fire of those days.
I am remembering faces I can no longer see.

And the places I loved that are gone from me
and the roads and the paths and the open ways,
I am burning the woods of my childhood, tree by tree.

Where the elm trees stood, where the fox ran free,
and we listened to the owl and the screeching jays,
I am remembering the faces I can no longer see.

For those who walked under the pines with me,
who cannot join me at the fire as I sit and gaze,
I am burning the woods of my childhood, tree by tree.

Thinking old dreams that no longer can be
Watching them fall into ashes, the reds into grays
I am remembering the faces I no longer can see.

While the fire goes low and night is around me,
the memory of that time rises up from the haze.
I am burning the woods of my childhood, tree by tree,
I am remembering the faces I no longer can see.

Two

Home to the Late Late Movie

This landscape like a supermarket aisle
draws me on. Flat and stocked
rows of suburbia, matchbox cars parked
in the driveways, frail little trees
strung tight and anchored to the yards.

And the snowmobiles rusting beside the garage,
and the chainlink fence with the shadow
lunging back and forth all morning, and the
plastic big-wheels on the graveled edge
of the road, white-blond hair of blue-eyed

Boys flirting with speed, pedaling their way
into traffic, looking over their shoulders
to the houses set uncertainly in the cornfields,
their mothers held captive by afternoon TV,
loneliness seeping through the vinyl blinds.

Until the fathers come home from the car shop,
from the lumber yard, from the freezer factory,
garage doors lifting, chains jerking in tracks,
the blond boys running across fat patches of grass,
the daughters glancing up from their books.

And sighs like ovens and the clatter of dinner
plates coming from kitchens, a sizzling in the pan,

stainless steel lifted to the mouth, the smoke of
conversations drifting from the chimneys, dissipating
over the gray branches of the leafless wind.

And later on these streets: in each house with
its drapes parted slightly, wafer of lamplight
caught on bare walls, blue of a video eye
flickering its gaze back into the night, the
refrigerators are opening, letting out the cold.

Solitaire

When there is too little love in the air,
cut out a moon and paste it into your heart.

And you can dance alone, especially on those gray
afternoons when you start listening to a woman

Singing, and she knows how to twist the notes and
get you singing along with her like a diamond shook

From its wedding band, lost on a gravelly beach where
every grain of sand doesn't pay you any attention.

If there is something you are trying to forget,
go out and buy an exotic plant and watch it

Resist your attempts to drown it in your
solicitous care. Make sure this plant is

Something that will bloom: a hibiscus or an orchid.
And if you are ever lonely and have to walk home alone,

Pretend that the phone is ringing and that you won't
get there in time. Tell yourself that all the letters

That were meant for you are in a gray sack at the
back of the biggest post office in America.

Remember playing cards at your grandmother's table:
the two of you laying down your separate and solitary hands.

Mr. Muse

I have a muse, he calls me collect,
from a different city every time.
I never know where to reach him.
He makes me want to bring him home,
but I always have more to say
after he goes away.

He listens for the part of me
that no one else believes is there.
He never pays the bills,
but he is funny without even trying.

I have a muse, he calls me into the
present with the scent of camomile
rubbed between his finger and thumb.
Smell this, he says.
His feet are leafy,
his eyes are like the clouds.

Sometimes he is gone for months.
Maybe he collects unemployment;
maybe they think his work is seasonal.
Maybe he is in treatment;
maybe he's got the blues.
I don't know where he goes;
I just know I miss him
and start to watch the roads
for someone who comes whistling along

in the late afternoon.
I start expecting to see him
sitting on the front step one morning
with something amazing in his arms
— whatever it is that muses bring.

The Beginnings of Philosophy

The old man Socrates
is half wrapped in the blankets
of his Greek bed, and surrounded
for once, by a crowded house.
Greece is screaming with vultures.

Already he has divided things:
empty, half-full, and filled.

Hemlock is the elixir of truth.
And so he passes away
and leaves us with Plato.
Plato likes to sit in McDonald's
and watch the teenagers smoke cigarettes.
He likes the way they lean over
each other.

The pipes of knowledge tremble,
as if they have been charged
with a new substance.

Her back is all that Aristotle
can see — a small triangle of
almost pink. He knows then that
he won't follow in the footsteps
already hardening on the rock.

The globe spins around on its axis
and comes to rest under her
small fingers.

Skip the introduction.
There are a hundred ways to begin.

From Out the Cave

When you have been
at war with yourself
for so many years that
you have forgotten why,
when you have been driving
for hours and only
gradually begin to realize
that you have lost the way,
when you have cut
hastily into the fabric,
when you have signed
papers in distraction,
when it has been centuries
since you watched the sun set
or the rain fall, and the clouds,
drifting overhead, pass as flat
as anything on a postcard;
when, in the midst of these
everyday nightmares, you
understand that you could
wake up,
you could turn
and go back
to the last thing you
remember doing
with your whole heart:
that passionate kiss,
the brilliant drop of love

rolling along the tongue of a green leaf,
then you wake,
you stumble from your cave,
blinking in the sun,
naming every shadow
as it slips.

Lunar Landing

It was morning on the day
of the first moon walk,
and the whole sky turned black.
The earth was drifting weightlessly
into space, tethered to a crackling
voice, to mission control, NASA calling.
We, watching, were all unwieldy in our progress
as we lumbered across the new universe
with stiff and graceless gait, our arms
half-limp at our sides, our fingers
monstrously gloved, our faces blown away
under the black mask of reflected space.

Earlier that week, I went into Nova Scotia,
far away from the jittery jubilation
of patriotic hype, the ponderous tones
of network newsmen on that historic occasion,
that one small step for man, that giant leap
for mankind.

I left the country on purpose,
shedding my presence like a red, white,
and blue skin, unfurling my freakish banner along
the Bay of Fundy, as I watched the mile-long tide streaming
over morning gold sand,
pulled by that moon,
    by that moon
        that moon

I saw the night before
round and untouched by human hand,
the bare, blue-white breast of night
shining in the blanketed bed of stars,
like an ancient Lucrece, sleeping
in the never before disturbed
bower of space, while this new Tarquin
hurtled soundlessly toward her,
intent on leaving his imprint,
determined to plant his flag,
and abandon her, forever marred,
the red and white of his colors
bleeding in the blue video
of his conquest.

Of Thee, I Cannot Sing

There's no way to make that place
sound like a postcard. Fifty years ago,
even more, Scott Fitzgerald called it
the ugliest place he had ever seen:
rows of oil refineries, steel-skinned
bridges rusting across the brown sludge
of a river, the sky sweating over the
hollow-eyed buildings, the billboards
faded and peeling, fields of glass and
skeleton cars, streets gouged and buckled,
unmarked, untraveled except by the low
trolling shadows of pushers and pimps.
That's where we met you, Billy of the War,
when you'd just come back from Vietnam
with your story about how the army
was the only way out, how it kept you
out of jail, out of the family business,
and sent you to the beautiful land,
hurled into the sky, splayed
on the hot ripple of the wind,
and let you drift to the jungle's floor.
There, in a green glade, breathing in
the country air, red dirt under your feet,
you didn't worry when the planes
buzzed overhead, didn't realize
that dust, drifting down to where

you crouched under the palm leaves
was poison from the same dirty fucked-up
machine that wrecked the city back home,
that diabolic mix of greed and stupidity
sending you from one corner of hell to another.

Grand Canyon, Early December

There they are on the North Rim
of the Grand Canyon. Notice that
his hair was longer than hers.
It was almost Christmas, and
they thought they might drive up
to St. Paul after they had a look
at this archipelago, this purple-
throated ocean of canyon and cliff.
It was cold and they slept
along the way, entirely avoiding L.A.
(they had never been to there
and liked saying that they didn't care).
Just outside of San Francisco,
they picked up a hitch-hiker
and took him along to somewhere
past Needles, Arizona. It's hard
to remember now, but it seems they had
to turn over some food at the state line:
tomatoes? apples maybe? They filled
the gas tank and drove along the blue-black
highway until they felt pulled to that place.
He stood for a long time on the rim
in that way he had: close to the edge,
zenlike in his solitude. (Oh, if she
had only taken this as a warning,
but her motto then was to ignore all clues,
make all moves as randomly as possible,
and never try to understand.) The view was,

she thought (and knew the echo), satisfactory:
the glass and silver river snaking through the
canyon bottom, the sun dissolving into
the layered rock, the violet-tinged
gorge of scar that made her wonder:
What meteor was it slammed its fiery fist
into earth's smooth face? What terrible,
titanic angel reclined his limbs
in the slaking, new-made planet
and beat his pinioned wings
deep and deeper into the rock?

Canyon

And I, who feared the ledge, the rim, the scrimmed edge,
where you would stand, storklike, your right foot
resting on your left

As you looked out, over the vast and deep canyon,
the titanic expanse of rainbowed rock,
I now do this high-wire act,

Learning to center my weight over the sag of thin line,
willing myself into the clenched pose of one
who walks without a net.

To do this is a kind of craziness — I wrench forward
with every step, too frightened to see
the birds flying under my feet,

Deafened by the roar of blood in my ear, I cannot
hear your voice telling me to touch the clouds.
I do not touch the clouds.

Gravity fills my bones and runs in my veins.
Descending, I taste time, layer by layer.
It tastes like nothing.

Now I can meditate upon the barren bones of the years,
the purple of gaudy days, sinking into
the hourglass of ocean

Stretching farther than horizon, moving with
motionless crashing, the wisest wave
that never breaks.

Only a whisper comes back to the ledge
where I remember how I walked on air,
the future underfoot.

Great Salt Lake

The clouds on the horizon brought
a storm later that night, but here
they are lovely, rubbing their dark
knuckles over the yellow dunes,
flickering slivers of lightning
into the sage-green water.
Plagues of midges sweep the salt-white beach;
coppered snakes swirl in the silken lake.

Still we go in. We make this one
pilgrimage, and though we try to sink,
we stay afloat. We sit cross-legged
in the water, supported by ropy
fingers that leave ghost traces
on our skins. We think we hear
a choir singing. Eventually, we grow
tired of skimming the surface
and wash the brine from our bodies.

Night, we roll into sleep
and dream of coyotes, of rattlers,
of door handles breaking off
in our hands, the brittle
chrome of our first fears.

Rural Route 2

When we moved back, Midwest, we lived out of town
in a house built on a century of cornfields,
the old layers of stalk and stubble packed deep,
a tangled mat of alfalfa woven between.
In spring, the fields woke beneath us, rocks
groaning toward the surface, desperate to break
their granite teeth through the plowed skin
of land, ready to cover the hills like manna.
But the green lawn, thatched with rolls of sod,
watered without cloud or thunder, kept them down.

The house itself was something I could circle twenty
times and still miss the way in. It was deceptive
and smooth like a gravestone, like a mirage on the road.
Every time I tried to walk away from it, it brought me
back again. Sitting there, I couldn't let my heart go,
the string of it wound tight around my wrist.

Fishing New York

Here, while dogs bark
in the bottle-green air
of lonely, I hold my pen
like a three-barbed hook
tied to the reel of thoughts
drifting through
the deep of me.

Away
the flickering
nylon goes,
from out my
winding heart,
and I
wonder what I might
catch: what baited
revelation
might I haul
into this, my
rocking.

When I sleep,
I dream the city.
I put a finger
in its gray navel
and peel away the skin.
When next I touch,

trees and birds
erupt through
the cement.
I make a stringer
of the things I catch.

Coil and Halt

While I struggled with the memory of a woodpile, the late
afternoon got its skinny fingers around the day's throat
and tried to choke out the sun.

Earlier I was beautiful, and the world was spinning
smoothly. Jewel-eyed in the dark, cinnamon-scented,
I drifted with this.

But gaunt creatures were pawing the shrinking snows.
Over the hills, the sap was running in the trees.
Spring, I assumed.

Goliath was the shadow of things on my mind. Also
known as Giant Despair, Behemoth of the Deep, Leviathan,
he had me surrounded.

It bothered my sense of symmetry to notice how a perfectly
unplanned life could take on such an intricate pattern.
It made me nervous.

I looked out of my window, just at sunset,
saw a roof, heavy with snow, collapse under the evil sky.
It took less than a second.

Three

Announcing Augie

Begun in the headless hours of dawn,
to drift in the embryonic sea.
Begun for an ever,
come forth the one day
which was birth;
Augie, with a sharp tooth
curled his tiny footprints,
his precious finger swirls
tighter, and tight,
so that only he
could know his name.
The inky nurse-pad
called the doctor from his needle.
Augie showed his one tooth,
Augie spit into his eye.
So the doctor called the chaplain
who carried prayers of ether
in his shirt sleeves.
Augie bobbed in the mist,
trying to see beyond his mound of mother.
As they pulled his fingers flat,
as they pressed his fingers down,
Augie dreamt himself a circle,
where palm and sole united.

Not Quite Born Again

Augie lacerated himself with broken morning.
The moon, falling from the trees
had shattered into a clutter of light
along the horizon.
He was a locust,
dragging his body into death;
a snake,
who comes forth from the old skin
erasing his new tenderness
with the grit of day.

Civil Defense

Just as the thunder cracked,
just as the hail stoned down,
    while his father cadillacked,
    his cigaretted mother planted,
    brother crouched on the basement landing,
Augie,
dressed in the rags of a self-
investigation,
pressed into
the north-northwest
corner of his basement.

Self-Defense

Hiii-yuh!
Foot bare menace,
corduroy leg uncoiling.
HuH! eeeh! HuH!
Augie kicks his love into the fireplace.
uhhhh! HA!
The slow bricks of love
shatter.

Against Decay

In October,
Augie climbed a crimson maple tree
and gathered its leaves
one by one.
That took all the month
and he could not answer his telephone.

Then, in November, Augie went to the library.
He took his sacks of scarlet leaves
and pressed each one into a book.
That took all the month
and her letters went unanswered.

All winter, Augie thought of his tree
now safely stowed inside the library
and of the foolish wind
knocking
in vain.

Augie, Walking in January

Cold winter, the mangy thing!
Cruel winter, the bitter hag!
    Thus Augie lashed with his tongue
    as around the corner he slumped,
    sour expression ready for those who
    met him
    head on.

This is the way the cold delays.
This is the kindness before decay.

Cold winter, yet dear winter
to wring such grayness
from the earth !
    Thus Augie more mildly
    faced the avenue.

Augie Keeps Godot Waiting

Always,
extenuating circumstances
kept Augie from evolving
into an
existentialist.
Dear Mr. Godot, he wrote,
I'm sorry I did not keep
my appointment with you.
I thought I'd buy a farm,
or that my father would die,
but none of these things
happened. However,
I have finally found a girl
even my mother could love,
a girl who will join my revolution.
At night she lies crucified to the bed:
a rose of many thorns
for me to embrace.
Perhaps I will come
when this is over.

Augie on the North Shore

Cedar fingered and birch torn,
the long gaze of moonlight.
He stands in tree,
shadowed,
clouds away the bright eye.
The swift smoke of his mind
sifts through
the moaning wood.

Out on the bare rock of planet,
he finds the inland sea
shifting its hoard of stones.

The fog seeps from the diamond willow swamps,
the honeycomb of water and land
behind him.
Serpentine the trail to the north.

Quiet at last,
he sees the ghost of great trees
rising from the harbor.
Up the Gunflint Trail,
a wolf paces,
hesitates,
then leaps
the still warm trail of human passing.

The Old Extreme

I will not go to Vietnam, said Augie, and
you can't make me.
Nothing you say will make me go.
No matter how you beg and plead
I will not go.
I'll hold my breath until I'm purple.
I'll lie on the floor and kick my feet.
I'll lose forty pounds.
I'll get a psychiatrist.
I'll bang my elbows together.
I'll bang my head against the wall.
I'll change my name.
I'll change my heartbeat.
I'll hear things you don't hear.
I'll see what you don't see.
I'll become a dope addict.
And, if that doesn't work
I'll scream all night long,
wet my pants,
and eat cockroaches.
But personally,
I'd rather not go
to such extremes.

Lottery 1969

Oh the green of the moon
and the silvery trees,
the stars in the lake
and the big waves of night.

Augie rowed by in a double brass bed.
Augie rowed by with a gun to his head.

Past the bandshell square
where an old monk was chanting,
through the green park
with its long rows of crosses.

Augie shouted down from the wings of his pigeon,
He looked for pennies in the wishing wells.

For in the blood of night
a hand picked the numbers
by the light of the newsroom,
they set Augie free.

Augie and the Pentecostals

First the red-faced Colonel Sanders man
shook his hand.
Good Morning, Brother Augie!
Hallelujah!
Then they sang:
not like an organ,
not seraphic.
They sang like tin cans in the sun
and shouted and prayed
in red woolen voices
and moaned like
trees falling.
And in their wind
and storm,
Augie,
feeling
(for once)
out-numbered,
fled
the congregation.

Prayer For

Augie Marino has fallen away.
He's degenerate and rude
and wants to stay that way.

So? Leave him alone
and perhaps he'll come home.
(There's a little sheep in all of us.)

Four

Holland Park at Dusk

Across the gardens — where one shade of green
layered itself against another darker and
still another lifted its frosted almost blue
green to the palest yellow — there was a peacock on the wall,
his unearthly call breaking the flutter of sweeter wings.
Excellent birds in the overleafing sky.

I don't know how the sun, a brightness
hidden behind the peacock's wall, filled the
chestnut leaves, or how each seven-rayed
cluster shadowed bright in the evening breeze,
but I saw how deeply those pieces of the world
held up the spaces between each other.

I heard a clarinet, playing "Darling Where Is Your Heart?"
and three men talked of springtime and parted
one by one. Children played under the trees.
Grandmothers walked. Even when the man from the café
came out with his broom and swept up the day —
even then, I couldn't move away.

Near the British Museum

Russell Square is littered
with pigeons and candy wrappers.
The inverted fountain
bares its cracked navel to the sky,
and a man in a turban settles
between the ancient roots.

Over by the café, a woman
reads a sentence or two
then pauses when a flood
gathers behind her eyes,
the crest reached long ago,
now inching over her heart.

A block from her coffee cup,
pieces of the Parthenon
hug museum walls,
a weight of marble sculpted,
even as she is,
in various positions of agony.

She thinks of the shapes
in the Egyptian Hall,
and of their smooth faces,
of crocodiles and the Nile's flood,
the promise of fields after
the effortless scattering of seed.

In the Distant Dark

Sometimes I listen to news
from your part of the world
as it arches over the Atlantic,
bounces off satellites
and catches me in the darkness.
The digital numbers on my
clock-radio pulse as
if to say that 12:55 is a lie,
that over there, where the day
has already filled the sky,
the real world is beginning,
that the truth is 6:55
in Greenwich, where
the *Cutty Sark* nestles up
against a cement dock,
and water drips in the tunnel
under the Thames, and people
walk slowly across the prime meridian.
Time is really happening there.
Time is taking a train
to Central London, reading
any one of the papers —
headlines of which this voice
is telling me now, how they
were emerging from the station
when the bomb exploded,
how they felt it long after
the light climbed higher.

69

Riding East to Dover

From our window we saw the yellow rapefields
covering the plains of Kent and drank
our filtered coffee and ate our Bramley
pies. Kent, sir — everybody knows Kent:
Apples, cherries, hops, and women, said Mr.
Jingle. And still the hopfields, and still
some ancient oast houses, their cone hats
surprising the horizon. My companion, affable
but complaining of filmy windows, stretched
his legs and noticed the oak trees downed by
winter storms, predicted the deforestation of
the few remaining treestands in Britain, was
gleeful despite his visions, cheered by
the prospect of imminent derailment, or at
least a long halt just outside of some paint-
blistered town on the Kentish Downs, where little
back gardens shouldered up to each other, glass
houses sheltering clay pots, rakes, and hoes
glinting dully, the cement crumbling into weeds.

Somewhere, Close to Dover Beach

Such words they speak together:
stone upon stone, laid in some fieldy wall.
They let the moon and clear sky
wander through the branches.
They have a winter love.

Such silences are heaped between them:
white cliffs that rise majestically,
something for the last light to glint upon;
listen, you hear the grating roar and yes,
the planet's shoals and shingles are visible.

Such pain they have, making them
almost too weary to speak, but they do,
coming to the window in this, the aftermath
of their private wars, ignorant armies
having clashed, senseless incertitudes spilled
into what could have been kind
night air, coming to them in waves,
another shore always beckoning, and sometimes
after the again and yet again
— the long droned sorrow passed —
they turn and say such words:
Ah love . . .

Reading Sylvia Plath in London

You frighten me.
It is hard to read your words,
and hear the stories of black London days:
the desperate mix of hope and hate,
the never quite right way to live,
and always, aren't we to blame?
Nothing enough or close to perfect
except for, possibly, describing
the coldness of the kill or the peaceful cruelty
of a self-inflicted final scene, which
still unravels and comes back,
enshrouded and laserlike
in a trail of confusion,
wearing out the soul
with its weary chant:

> Deliver us from
> warm milk,
> from chipping paint,
> the gas-blue flame,
> the hiss,
> the hum,
> the sinking eye,
> gray morning fog.

And now the Thames to the south,
the Tower and ravens to the east,
and your words spreading
over the Unreal City,
a deeper shade of
grief.

Tapping the Lid

Oh she was clever, never doubt it
and could tell a hawk from a handsaw.
Her mother may have been even more
talented, but she lacked advancement.
These things have a way of being told
and never come out right in the end
no matter how many breaths you hold
or stars are wished upon, it all ends
flat on the page in a hospital gown.
We know then the exact dosage
and even read the transcripts of
desultory conversations, the yesses
and uhhumms, we imagine the drums
beating or the fires burning only
evidenced by the traces in the EKGs
or the notebooks that won't be published
for a half-century, thankyouverymuch
and by that time the others will have
had their say, having been interviewed
for the documentary, voices over the
London rooftops, her silhouette at the
cooker, her fingers lingering on the
milk bottle. In a week or two
they will attempt to reconstruct
the site of her destruction,
to broadcast her whisper to the ears
of the whole wide world, she

who is now so quiet in her coffin
listening to the sound of bees
in a hive, paying attention to
that mysterious line that divides
the ocean from the storming sky.

Elegy

for Sylvia Plath

O Lady Lazarus, my Lady Hamlet, come back from the dead,
trailing your fingers in the shadow you leave,
making the edges of words meet in a tear-brimmed eye:
you speak the souls of dreams, remembering everything.

You walk out of your grave into the air
where dusty death makes its equivocation with veins —
all of this to be of some use to the flowers,
and to the trees who drink you into their leaves.

Now you can recite your father's death, forgive
the shabbiness of his burial and disdain the poor worms.
Now you can push aside this nut-shelled world,
the stream of linen floating from your uplifted arms.

You bring a burning joy inexplicable and then
a heart scraped bare — happiness all pinched shut.
Still, I want to keep you alive, keep the breath moving
in and out, out and in, like an ocean's green lung.

The Famous Poet's Grave

At the famous poet's grave we paused,
startled by the plain white cross in
a hill that sloped, the long grasses
curling in the wind, rolling under the
sea-gray skies. Walking out along the
path from the castle, I tried to tell
you about villanelles and the dying of
the light, but truthfully I was
thinking more of a story by a woman
who came to the poet's grave with a
man she was about to leave and how
they stayed in a room somewhere over
there in the town that the poet
walked to each late afternoon, ready
to take up his bottle and talk.

How the Puritans Took London

I can still feel the sadness, sinking into me,
a descending platform carrying some
wrapped-up thought of you: going down,
going down, until I feel no more.

I liked the fact that you could recite
poetry by heart — very few people can these days.
And you knew a good slate when you saw one,
though you couldn't hang a shelf to save your life.

I confess that I only remember the name of one
of those flowers we loved. Thrift, dear Horatio,
thrift: that pink flower that grows in clumps
along the Cornish Coast. Remember me.

Sometimes, I am fiercely angry at you. All that
distance drags through my veins, and pulls me asleep
in weedy Lethean waves. I dream about Ophelia
wandering through the Tate and out to the Thames.

On the steps, she stops for ice cream and goes down
to dance with the witches at the National. In the end,
that pitiful platform rises again, its gallows hungry
for our hearts. Good-bye, we say, and London floats away.

Waiting for You

I am waiting on the shadow's edge. The moon,
building a tower of whiteness, frightens me.
I look up telephone numbers,
I open the curtains, turn off the lights.

Away past the street lamp,
past the circle of my voice,
a door is slamming in the wind.
Come home, I whisper.

Every second is a departure.
Wrappers are scuttling across the platform,
the last train slips into its black tunnel.
I am waiting. I know all the posters by heart.

Then I hear a catching throb of song. Some party.
Voices pushing at each other in the dark,
then fading. Someone's footsteps on the sidewalk,
dog-collar jingle. A bit of wind.

Out of Orbit

After you go away from me,
I hang onto the planet
as the days and then the years
go by. The distances between
our nights and days lengthen
and then disappear. The moon
falls over the edge of your absence,
and loses her heart.

Trees come out of the sky
and are erased by things
that once surrounded their too
too solid limbs. I lean into
the earth, trying to see
the nothing that comes of
something as important
as our love once seemed.

Eventually, I talk
about you as someone
who will never return.
I give away the dreams
we dreamed together
and pretend you are
like any glimmer
on the horizon,
deceiving me
into believing

that you would be here
in this place that I
could see in the
distance: this empty
and endless orbit,
where everything
is just out of
anyone's reach.

The Plaza

The empty-eyed and hollow-hearted
linger along the edges of a fountain

feeding pigeons and smoking cigarettes.
They hear the whine of trucks on the

distant freeway, they sense automatic
garage doors opening in the suburbs.

Top 40 hits pass through their bones and
leave traces. They hum the mindless melodies

of advertising jingles, slogans loop through
their brains, slicing off sections of silence,

strangling the thought that almost surfaced.
All the while they are hoping for some sort

of salvation, some sign that they are only
lost temporarily. They think that they would

welcome a prophet if she came, her hair wild
under a baseball cap, fingernails chewed, no

fashion sense. That man who slides down from
his office and stands looking up at the silver

and glass-scrapered sky, tie drifting in the
breeze, black car reflected in his sunglasses,

does he suspect that she might have his answer?
Or is he looking for some Einstein bum, who

stumbles against the light, talking dirty
to the payphone and reciting parts of Milton?

Does he want that face on the billboard, polished
and posed in a gaze of steady invitation, ready

to tell him everything and its lonely echo?

Edgar's Dream

And always I can imagine myself back
into that part of London, as if
coming up the steps of the Underground
and turning into the quick familiar street,
the mail pillar thick with red paint,
birds settling on the window ledges,
even flying into our kitchen to eat crusts,
flapping against the sunlit floor and then
back out to the narrow street, the bluest
skies in three centuries between the rooftops.

Sunday afternoons in the park, watching
the rowers and the peacock's spreading
their plumes when I leaned over the rail.
Walking the path under chestnut trees,
people resting on the benches,
dogs, children, cricket on the green,
shouts floating overhead like kites,
the pleasure of walking under the arch
where teenagers listened to Pink Floyd.

I hoped they would remember me, my notebook
and cappuccino, how I sat for hours watching
the children feed pigeons, indulgent in

this life across the globe, always careful
not to lose myself or stand too close to the edge
of the conjured up cliff, where I could see
fishermen, small as mice on the beach below
and the birds wheeling halfway down.

Five

Death Becomes Me

Death has been checking me out,
making himself at home in my body,
as if he needed to know his way
through the skin, faintly rippling
over the cheekbone to the hollow
beneath my eyes, loosening
the tightly wound ligaments
in the arm, the leg,
infirming the muscle
with his subtle caress,
traveling along the nerve,
leaping from one synapse
to the next, weaving his dark threads
into the chord that holds me tall.
Death is counting my hair,
figuring out the linear equation
of my veins and arteries,
the raised power
of a million capillaries,
acquainting himself with the
calculus of my heart,
accessing the archives
of memory, reading them
forward and backward,
finding his name everywhere.
Death comes to rest in my womb,
slaking away the rich velvet
of those walls, silently halting

the descending pearls,
as if he could burrow in
and make himself my mother,
as if he could bare my bones
and bring me to that other birth.

Suppose Death Comes Like This

Suppose it is the sound of a window opening,
the scrape of wood against wood and the
weight dropping along the groove in the sash,
glass rattling in the frame? Or suppose
it is a man, coughing in the other room,
the rasp of his throat sawing through
the thin wall, there, just above the mirror?
Or suppose it is a telephone ringing
from the house next door, and the blur
of bird wings crosses silently through it?
Or an engine overhead, riding unevenly
in thick clouds, a steady hum coming on
so gradually? Suppose you fail to hear it?
Suppose it is as unportentous as that?

Memento Mori

Beneath the skin, a grinning skull,
a skeleton buried in muscle and flesh.

I close my eyelids over the gape of socket,
over the now tender jelly of sight.

Open jawbone. My bite, cross-winged and yellow,
is chattering its distinctive disarray.

I'm sifting through the essence of mortality,
the obscured remains of what I will be.

One day, this room I inhabit,
this tower I carry on weary shoulders

May rest in someone's hand — held out at arm's length,
and then a voice, contemplating the airy degrees of faceted

Bone, will consider what dust I am become, and nothing of these
      thoughts, this thick
inhabited world, this vast

Ceiling of sight and song — nothing of this
will disturb the pulse of that fragile meeting.

Last Duet

I start out alone, in one of Bach's inventions.
On the second page, where my fingers
do not know the way as well, I slow
the notes down, and a few measures later
I leave the page, as the fourth finger
of each hand discovers a resonance that
must be repeated, a harmonic that echoes
in the hollow bone. From then on, my hands
find their own places to go, as natural
as walking through the woods without a path,
as easy as one wanders, absorbed by the shore,
looking for shells and sea glass.

On the corner of the music ledge,
a pot of crocus blooms. I translate
its purple and green into arpeggios,
thinking of botanical gardens, where
daffodils push through the grassy stretches
between tall trees silvered over with
winter, the promise of rhododendrons
hidden in the left hand, the certainty
of lilacs and cherry blossoms in the right.

Above this music of petal and stem,
the patina of dark wood glows like a coffin,
the edge of crocheted cotton lifts, the name
of the piano company in gold letters
rises over my knuckles, that old marquee

of a thousand imaginary performances.
I dreamed I chiseled out my own epitaph and that
one by one, the letters broke out of the stone
like new-hatched birds, their wings opening.

Though it is evening, a light is in me
as I play, the trace of sunned winter
snow, the reflection of this coming into
the bare window of a room where there is
only a piano. My lost cousin comes
and plays duets with me, as his mother taps
the measures with her large rough hand.
Our bodies touch so slightly, hip and elbow,
all four hands together again in the light.

Dreaming You Out of Honduras

for Miguel

At night, when you go to sleep,
floating over wooden floors
in a bed of pale snowlight,
the future comes to you
dressed in a hundred orchids,
sheen of mahogany skin,
the fragrance of orange trees.

When you are there
it will be as they say —
the dark stillness of Lake Yojoa
under the shoulders of purpled mountains.
Turistas will haul black fish into their boats,
tiny white skiers will skim
the slow waters of alligator.
You might see the giant boa
that lives on the mountainside
waiting to eat cattle and jungle deer.
Oxcarts will pass by, carrying melons and firewood,
up and over the Sierra Espíritu Santo.

But in this dream I've made for you,
the jungle grows backward
and uncovers the stones of Copán,
where the Bat God of Twilight
hangs upside down from the stars
and carves blank-eyed statues into the mountain.

The skulls and bones of old conquerors
await the black expanse of pirate flags,
coming through the centuries
to anchor in the Bay Islands.

In this dream the ceiba tree
rises above the jungle.
Climbing to the peak, you see
into the dark plagues of Europe,
and back to the fires of Rome
— even to the broken walls of Jerusalem.
When you fall from the heavens
into the twisted roots of today,
you wake,
loving only orchids.

What You Wanted

And when you finally find what you want,
they say, please allow six to eight weeks
for delivery, and then while you are waiting
you forget what you ordered or decide that
after all you could have lived without it.

When it comes, you leave it unopened
in the front hall for months.
It gathers dust and gets in the way,
but after a certain amount of time
it is far too late to send it back.

Reluctantly, you start to open it.
Somehow you manage to get one of the staples
stuck deep in your thumb; it draws a tunnel
of purple-blue blood up to the wound.
It hurts — a lot. You need a knife

to cut through the tape over the box flaps,
and as you sink the blade in
you feel like a hapless magician, hoping
that those who planned this magic trick
knew exactly what they were doing.

A Kind of Deliverance

Now my life opens, as suddenly
as the green that blurs across
the land in April, prodigious
as a magnolia flower, emerging
from the wand of the magic branch.

I will not say this season is
without its own blend of cruelty,
bred out of countless dead fields,
out of that bare ruined choir
of the year. I will say

It comes on inexorably, like a
child descending the birth canal,
pushed forward by contracting circles
of muscle, molding the mother's
bone and skin to her swift passage.

And who can tell which body is
most helpless: whether it is the
small one, forced out of a warm
ocean where she was rocked in the
constant beat of her mother's heart,

Or whether it is the body that
felt the auger at work in her womb,

the nauseous wave as the cells divided
and spun themselves into fingerbuds and
the tiny black speck of an eye, when

After many months, she imagined
that this occupation would last forever,
that she would always have those tiny feet
dancing the walls of her belly, and that birth
would not come along with its fistful of keys.

In Quest of Agates

And I have walked on golden graveled roads
my head bent in search of the red agate,
alert for a pock-marked skin or the ripple
of ringed color split wide open. My feet scraped
out movement, my head swung from side to side,
sweeping, sifting through the ordinary limestone
the white quartz, the granite shards — all the
rocky way that was not the glorious, elusive agate.

And I have heard the sound of meadowlarks as
I walked, the song of the field arising from
the plowey black furrows, the fence posts
graying into the new spring grass. Moving
along my row with a planter's straight aim,
I have had time to see the red of willow wands,
the garter snake sunning on the rock, the boot print
in the soft ground along the edge of the road.

Poised above a summer's night, I have learned
to fall into the wingless body of sleep,
the sound of pebbles rattling in my joints,
my pockets filled with a stone-smooth heaviness.
I think to myself as I am drifting that
there are few people who find treasure in the road
without stumbling, without falling to their knees.

After Visiting the Oracle

It stilled all other voices; the old clamor
scattered along the path of its passing.
It overcame me with the passion of telling,
welling up, as it did, from the shame-filled deep.

I opened my ears to the empty "because"
into which all unspoken, unsayable things
had slipped, down the throat of my
thirsty years, into the beds of memory.

After that, I let in another listener,
who burned down the dilapidated barrier
of broken words, and started once more
the throbbing of an inner voice.

At first, there was a hand, then
a lip, then an eye.
Masklike, I looked out through a green evening,
remembering it as green, trembling the line of leaf,

Paying attention to the words
that came drifting, like
birds,
returning to the branch.

Household Muse

All morning, I nurse some fretful sorrow.
I take down curtains that gray at gathered
edges, I pull out dusty screens and wash
windows with blue water and newspaper,
the way my mother taught me. I throw
heaps of clothing into the middle of rooms:
jeans, sweaters, sweatshirts, dresses, belts,
underwear, old nylons — things no one ever
wears, things worn and ripped, things so
ugly I could not give them away. I stuff
these things into bags and boxes and carry
them out to a corner of the garage where
I won't have to look at them, hardly at all.
I go back into the house and sprinkle white
powder into the bathtubs and the sinks and
watch it blue over the rusty film of stainless
steel and porcelain. I pour a cap of piny
cleaner into an empty ice-cream pail; it
steams a vinegary smell, sloshes green and soapy.
Soon I have buckets everywhere: disinfectant
in the bathrooms, wood cleaner by the cabinets,
ammonia water for the walls. But then
the wind changes, and I am all of a sudden
weary and aware of this great effort
to wash the memory of love away. The muse

has departed, leaving me with afternoon.
My hands find no more places to scrub,
no more drawers to open; the light no longer
lifts the dust, and the house is abandoned,
like a page half-written, a rhythm that falters.

Living in the Body

Body is something you need in order to stay
on this planet and you only get one.
And no matter which one you get, it will not
be satisfactory. It will not be beautiful
enough, it will not be fast enough, it will
not keep on for days at a time, but will
pull you down into a sleepy swamp and
demand apples and coffee and chocolate cake.

Body is a thing you have to carry
from one day into the next. Always the
same eyebrows over the same eyes in the same
skin when you look in the mirror, and the
same creaky knee when you get up from the
floor and the same wrist under the watchband.
The changes you can make are small and
costly — better to leave it as it is.

Body is a thing that you have to leave
eventually. You know that because you have
seen others do it, others who were once like you,
living inside their pile of bones and
flesh, smiling at you, loving you,
leaning in the doorway, talking to you
for hours and then one day they
are gone. No forwarding address.

Crossroads

The second half of my life will be black
to the white rind of the old and fading moon.
The second half of my life will be water
over the cracked floor of these desert years.
I will land on my feet this time,
knowing at least two languages and who
my friends are. I will dress for the
occasion, and my hair shall be
whatever color I please.
Everyone will go on celebrating the old
birthday, counting the years as usual,
but I will count myself new from this
inception, this imprint of my own desire.

The second half of my life will be swift,
past leaning fenceposts, a gravel shoulder,
asphalt tickets, the beckon of open road.
The second half of my life will be wide-eyed,
fingers sifting through fine sands,
arms loose at my sides, wandering feet.
There will be new dreams every night,
and the drapes will never be closed.
I will toss my string of keys into a deep
well and old letters into the grate.

The second half of my life will be ice
breaking up on the river, rain
soaking the fields, a hand
held out, a fire,
and smoke going
upward, always up.

This book was designed by Wesley B. Tanner. The text was set in Sabon with Syntax for display by Wilsted & Taylor. The book was manufactured by Malloy Lithographing.